LETTING *Them* GO

STEPHANIE ASSELIN

This is a work of creative nonfiction. Some parts have been fictionalized in varying degrees, for various purposes. The conversations and events that took place in the book all come from the author's recollections. While all the stories in this book are true, some names and identifying details have been changed to protect the privacy of the people involved.

Copyright © 2022 by Stephanie Asselin

All rights reserved. No part of this book may be reproduced or used in any manner without written permission of the copyright owner except for the use of quotations in a book review. For more information, address: asselinsteph@hotmail.com

First paperback edition September 2022

Book design by Kamar Martin
Interior layout by Aalishaa

ISBN 978-1-7781694-1-0 (paperback)
ISBN 978-1-7781694-0-3 (ebook)

Table of contents

Preface v

Ducky 1

Coco 15

Cudi 21

Superman...31

Sasquatch 41

Marshmallow.. 73

Phoenix 81

If you made it into this book, Congratulations!
I loved you enough to write something about our time together.
Most of it isn't lovely, no sunshine and rainbows here.

Now, don't get me wrong, this book isn't dedicated to any of you.
It's dedicated to me. It's my way of washing my hands of our history.
The combination of poems and prose written in this book come from my 20s.
I can't let you take all the blame. I have hurt many of you equally.
I hadn't found my worth yet, and I was toxic as FUCK.
I found a way to love some aspect of every man that ever gave me the time of day.
Instead, I should have been loving myself, working on myself, and bettering myself.
I blame my daddy issues, which ultimately come from my mom.
(But that'll be for another book.)
I have forgiven you all and I have forgiven me.
This is also my way of forgetting.

But ask yourselves this...
Did I hurt you enough to write a book about it?

I fear that artists
As a whole
Know that the most beautiful artwork
Whether writing, song or drawing
Is delivered through pain and
Maybe, just maybe
We give in to bad situations,
In which we already know the outcome
Because
First, we are hopeful and
Second, because
we are artists.

Ducky

Maybe when we push people away
It's because, deep down, we know we're not ready for them or they're not ready for us.
Subconsciously, we know they're not good for us or we are not good for them.
Maybe when we push people away...
It's because they're meant to be pushed away.

LETTING THEM GO

So in love with the thought of being in love, you find yourself trying with every man.
Although good company isn't good enough,
a serious relationship isn't even in your five-year plan.
Too easily attached to the wrong ones, when Mr. Right came along, you ran.
And even if he chased after you, you would be screaming,
Catch me if you can.

I think we all need to start over sometimes. After every life-changing dark episode, I believe we need to take the time to remind ourselves that self-love is the most important love we have in life. After every lesson learned, I believe we need to take the time to get to know ourselves all over again and acknowledge the steps we're taking towards personal growth.
After every heartbreak
After every painful experience
After every low point in our lives
I believe we need to take the time to reflect on the things we must improve for our own self, to be the best person we can possibly be for ourselves.

It's the silence from a woman that you should fear rather than her words.
It's the silence of a woman that many should fear rather than her violent words.
The aggression in her tone will disappear into thin air
In one ear, out the other.
While every second of her silence is a dagger to the heart.
What is she thinking? What is she feeling?
You can try to assume her thoughts,
but you must comprehend that you cannot put words into an unspoken sentence.
Her silence speaks for itself.

It's the season of fallen leaves and failed dreams.

When tragedy strikes, we tend to fall apart at the seams.

Time and time again ...

Pen to paper, paper to pen ...

Self-help paperbacks in our bookshelves.

Funny how we are so quick to blame ourselves.

I hate when my mood doesn't match the weather.//
It's beautiful today, clear and blue.
Above 60 degrees and a little breezy.
I don't feel like dancing in my underwear.
But I open the windows because that's what you're supposed to do when it's the middle of spring.
I wake up at 9 am, but I force myself to sleep past noon.
Children playing outside, squirrels running after each other, birds chirping, happy-go-lucky melodies
It all does nothing for me.
I have a lingering headache that reminds me I should drink water, especially if I won't be eating.
I should at least wear my glasses, but today, I don't feel like doing anything right.

We attach ourselves too quickly to cheap words and minimal actions. It's ridiculous how easily we become so blind-sighted by those perfect words that sound like music to our ears.

Every time we remind ourselves, "Actions speak louder than words" and yet, we continue to dance to the music.

We're so captivated by these sweet-sounding rehearsed words, that with every new flesh entry into our lives, we'd like to believe that these words will be enough

That these words will fill in the steps of actions and these words will speak volumes more than any action they refuse to make.

LETTING THEM GO

You can't help someone get to first base if they're not even willing to bat.
Truthfully, I always get caught up in trying to save people.
As much as I know, and as many times as I have experienced it
I still try to help people who don't even try to help themselves.
Hoping that one day, I'll make them snap out of it.
But you can't force change upon someone who doesn't see the world the same way you do.

I remember every time I was in a meaningful relationship, I'd always get extremely upset when times would get hard and my significant other would just give up or we'd fight until we were drained of our energy, and we'd talk about breaking up. The reason why I would get upset is because my mentality was, "When times get hard, you don't just take the easy way out." With time, I noticed that the easy way out isn't breaking up. Walking away because you finally acknowledge the fact that your significant other isn't happy is hard. Walking away because you know that you're no longer happy is hard. Walking away because you finally realize that unfortunately you two are not meant to be is hard, mostly when love is still involved. The easy way out is staying together sometimes, anticipating the next fight, and convincing yourself that the relationship can work because "love can conquer all." Sometimes love isn't enough. If you two don't have a strong foundation built on trust and respect, you two will not work. If you two don't have good communication skills, you two will not work. If you two don't have a friendship, apart from your relationship, you two will not work. If you two don't want the same things, you two will not work.

Sometimes, you have to stop and ask yourself, "Am I taking the easy way out?"

Remember that thing you wanted, and life didn't give it to you, because it wasn't what you needed.

Look at you still wanting it and shit.

But the day life decides to give it to you as a test and you end up hurt, don't come crawling back here wondering why life would give you something so painful...

It isn't my job or my responsibility
To fix, help, save
Anyone.

Other than myself
I deserve more than someone who is broken.

I am not broken.

Is anyone out there?
Call me beautiful.
Despite my madness.
Within my madness.
I am beautiful.
My madness feels like rage.
A desire for the abnormal.
Unusual.
Unprecedented.
It isn't all messy, it isn't all anxiety.
It isn't all obsession and addiction.
It isn't all blood and bones.

I am more than my heart, my temptations.
The battles within me can fade.
I will still be beautiful.

Time and time again, you show me your true colors.
Time and time again, I pretend I am color-blind.

Coco

Your hands are at my throat.
I return the favor.
I stare into your hazel eyes.
I wonder if a father is supposed to watch the soul leave their child's body.
You let go, finally realizing what you've done.
I squeeze a little harder until your face turns a deep red.
I wonder if choking you should feel this normal.

LETTING THEM GO

I was a prisoner of you until I decided to forgive you.
But your blood runs through me, and
I am reminded that I can never escape you.

Don`t deprive someone of REAL love because you don`t know how to be REAL.

Cudi

It sucks when you try so hard, and you make so much of an effort for someone, and they don't make the same effort for you...

Instead of thinking, is he even worth it? I think to myself, am I even worth it for him?

Our self-worth is fundamentally at stake.

I used to be so focused on his happiness, I forgot about my own.

"As long as he's happy."

That's all that mattered.

The day I had dreaded to see
The day I had hoped you would have made an effort to see me.
Instead, it was someone who couldn't even own up to the scenery.
When we walked past Soupbol best believe, I thought to myself...
You and I are meant to be.
But it's a shame that you don't feel the same as me.
Now it's
"As long as I'm happy."

Last time you called and said you missed me, you just said that shit because you wanted pussy and you think calling your ex is a sure thing. Honestly, I don`t give a shit why you`re calling but you need to understand that I`m not a side chick. You will not fucking play with my emotions. Once upon a time you truly loved me, and you don`t fuck around with that just because you`re horny.

There comes a time when every single emotion that has been consuming you just aches to be divulged. But every nerve in your body locks into place to avoid word vomit. All you want to do is scream out exactly what you're feeling, without worrying about those two seconds at the end when you decide to shut up and allow what you just said to sink in enough to cause a reaction. And all you want to do is hug him, hold him, kiss him, lay with him, and even save him. But as much as you want to blurt everything out, you decide to swallow it. And as much as you want to do all those things, you don't dare reach out to him. Because you know that no matter what you say, no matter what you do...
It won't change how he feels about you.

I let so much shit pass with you. I literally played it dumb. You took advantage to do shit no one would have ever accepted because you knew how vulnerable I was. When I thought I hit rock bottom, you showed me that I could go lower. I was in a really bad place back then and you toyed with my emotions because I was an easy target. I was passive to multiple things that you were doing when quite honestly, I`m not a passive person at all. But I just wanted to be loved and I thought loving you would make you love me. I wasn`t in the right state of mind. My vision was blurry, and my heart was lonely. I forgot my worth, I forgot what I deserved, I forgot about myself. Nonetheless, since those awful days... I constantly remind myself to never forget about myself. It hasn`t been easy lately. But even if times worsen, I still remind myself that it`s only temporary. My strength only continues to grow with every tragedy I must overcome.

And I am proud to say, I overcame a tragedy.

Don't say you miss me,
when you're the reason why I'm no longer in your life.
You made your choice, and it wasn't me.
I predicted this day, the day you'd come back.
Just don't be surprised that my choice isn't you either.

*Sometimes, I wish you were such a constant...
that I`d never have to miss you.*

Superman

I come from a family of addicts.

Drugs.

Alcohol.

Gambling.

And I considered myself lucky when I didn't become addicted to drugs or alcohol, despite experimenting with both.

Until I met you.

I had no idea you could be addicted to a person.

I guess that's the gamble.

LETTING THEM GO

You traced my scars with your eyes at first
Like they were a fast-moving plane in the sky.
Fascinated.
Then you moved your fingers along the three-dimensional damaged skin
You hiked up my mountain of trauma
Swam into the depths of my mistakes.
You looked at me with questioning eyes, as if you couldn't imagine a beautiful girl with such an emotional past.
I laughed it off, "I was young and stupid."
But you won't accept my answer, my downplay, my shrug of a shoulder, and my weak attempt to lighten up the mood.
You grab me a little tighter.

"What the fuck is this?"
Frustrated.
I am confused, anxiety flooding in and I feel like your tight grip on my arm is a chokehold around my neck.
I need air and now I am reliving the first cut.
The skin opened ever so slightly.
The faint smell of blood.
The numbness of my body.
But my arm is not an advertisement for shame
And it's not a promotion for self-harm.
It is a town of healing.
A triumph.
A reminder that I overcame.

I am looking at myself in the mirror and I am
Satisfied.
You see this now.
You accept me as I am.

How can something so beautiful be so terrifying, all at the same time?
Love. Oceans. You.
The cool summer evening.
No one is around.
Dive my feet into the sand.
Wiggle my toes.
Walk closer to the edge.
The possibilities are endless.
But there must be a limit, right?
Watch the waves say hello.
Then goodbye.
The same way you did.
They come and go, but always return.
The same way love does.
The waves are encouraging me to join.
But I am so scared of being swept away.
The water surprises my feet.
Goosebumps all over.
My laugh is nervous but excited.
It's powerfully exhilarating.
Trust falls were never for me.
Leaps of faith were always my forte.
So I jump.
My heart jumps.
The water captures my whole body.
I forget I was ever afraid.
Until next time.

You were high and low.
Sweet and bitter.
Simple and complicated.
You were sugar on my lip that I kept tasting long after you were gone.
You were mint in the air, with a calming effect.
You were rollercoasters and movie dates.
You were high screams of laughter and dark nights filled with confessions.
I loved you all the same.
You let me into your aloof and gloomy allure, your dark mirrors showed a familiar face.
All at once, I was completely and utterly engulfed in your maze.

The familiar face was me.
I was looking back at myself.

There was fiery chemistry.
We would burst into flames every second of every minute we spent together.
Yet, we returned every time because at least we felt something.
Anything.
It always sparked.
It was always electric.
You learn to hate only when there isn't anything burning.

Once bitten, twice shy didn't apply to us.
Always bitten, ever curious.

I loved you because you set my mind aflame.
Thinking wasn't an option.
Feeling was the only outcome.

Some people leave your life, and some people leave footprints on your heart, I did both.
Some people leave your life, and some people leave footprints on your heart. You did both.

Sasquatch

I remember everything.
I remember the first time I saw you, I thought you were the most beautiful sunset.
Tall, dark, and handsome had a whole new meaning.
I remember you weren't in a good mood, but I tried my best to make you laugh.
I saw all your character in the gap between your two front teeth.
I remember asking you to repeat your name
3
4
5 times and I still didn't get it right.
Later, I found out you hated repeating yourself.

I remember your return, I was waiting for my lift, you were walking in the middle of the street. I thought, "Making a statement or suicidal?" But you walked with such confidence like the street belonged to you. You turned and recognized me. You shined your heart-melting smile in my direction, and I almost died right there and then.

The first time we hung out, you rushed and rushed to get to your game on time.
I met some of your friends. It's the night I learned your earth revolved around basketball and family. I learned you were only here for a quick summer visit because the waters were calling you back. I questioned if we had been cast in a movie without knowing we were the lead characters. We spoke for hours about life in general, and in specifics. How you ordered a sandwich, our ages, my tattoos, how many

siblings you had, my dream of going back to school, what you were studying in school, your aspirations, and my dreams.
Kiddo and Sasquatch...
Making new nicknames stick. I fell harder and deeper into the quicksand of our similarities and differences. The red caravan, the one that ended up being engraved in my memory for years ... wishing and wishing it was always you passing by.
It happened once.

That first night, your car needed a boost, in the middle of the night.
What time is it?
1
2
3 am.
A guy was nice enough to notice we were in trouble.
Except I had known hours ago, we would be in trouble if this connection between us intensified. You wanted to drive me home, I declined ... you insisted. I let you. I asked if you wanted to come in, you were tired and driving - a deadly combination. You accepted.
It intensified.

It wasn't about the sexual tension, but something so much harder to find.
You proved to me that I wasn't the only one engulfed in this electricity. We were both on our sides, barely knowing each other, yet being so familiar in this space. We were turned away but still felt invisible ropes pulling us together.

You knew I was thinking hard about what was going to happen once you left, how this could possibly be the beginning of something and yet the end of everything. You pointed out the heaviness in the air and I couldn't grasp how you knew without me saying a word. Being around you felt like floating in ocean waters and letting the desire of the current take you completely in its fateful direction, knowing getting lost in your waves was the safest I'd ever been.

LETTING THEM GO

I think you were always meant to crawl into the empty spaces that I saved for a rainy day. As darkness falls, and my mood matches the skies _ you'd be the lighthouse seen from across the deep waters. I don't think I'd be ready to let go of you yet _ when you've lived without color for all these years, and someone comes into your sacred place with a paintbrush to splash light into your life...

you appreciate it more than all the times people took sledgehammers to your walls.

Light the letters on fire with your burning rage.
A wolf with blood dripping down its face.
I'm here like, "hurt me, hurt me, hurt me."
What a tragedy, just for a fucking muse.
It'll all be over soon.
All the poems, conversations _
They were a work of art
In the process of ripping out my own heart.

LETTING THEM GO

I can't fathom the idea of closing my eyes and you not being there.
The day you disappear is the same day I lose my footing.
Forever hoping I'd find my balance again.
Still flabbergasted by what you do to me.
How the days led to weeks to months and then years _
Years later and you're still here.
Stuck in a part of me that I can't dig out
No matter how hard I scratch.
Even if I lose a part of myself in the process, an irreplaceable void I'd be willing
You're like a scab that never heals, a constant reminder of my struggles and pain.
The love that never was but always will be.
They said there are three sides to every story:
Mine, yours, and the truth.
So, what's ours?
I wonder if we are consistent
If our stories align like they've been rehearsed.
I pride myself on being honest but when it comes to you,
You're my best-kept secret.
My forbidden desire, the one I can't have but so strongly crave.
The nights are long but trust me, the detox is longer.

What would have happened?
If you showed up to say bye _
If you weren't so drunk _
Had you kept to your slurred words _
Would I have loved him the same?

You're an enigma.
Everyone you cross paths with is stuck trying to figure you out.
If I could study anyone or anything, you'd be my favorite subject _ no doubt.
You're the experiment, the lab rat, the doctor, the apparatus, the teacher and
you're beside me in the audience.
You're everywhere, like a panic room, no matter which way you turn
There's no escape.
You're the serial killer everyone wants to undrape.
You're the math problem no one can solve.
You're the relationship that ended so abruptly.
You're the lost loved one, turned angel, too early.
There's a secret door in every compartment with a special key.
The more answers we get, the more questions grow.
The more you know, the more you realize how much you don't actually know.
You're a chameleon that keeps changing colors.
The snake that keeps shedding his skin.
Every time someone gets close to understanding _
You go through a metamorphosis.

I feel a gravitational pull towards you
And I don't know how to tell my atoms to stop vibrating in your direction.
Maybe I'm just soaking it all in before I build up the courage to walk away.
Be brave enough to never look back.
Maybe a part of me knows _
If I disappear, you wouldn't try to find me.
You'd say you respected my wishes
While I'd search the ends of the earth just to feel you once more.
Just to write the last poem.
It's difficult knowing that I'd only be writing from a retrospective point of view
From that moment on.
Sometimes our memory is distorted _
Sometimes you have to be standing in the pool of profound emotion to get the best recall.
The love, the friendship, the conversations
I imagine that at one point, it'll all fade
And be replaced by new feelings, new connections, new discoveries.
Perhaps, there will always be a part of me that will miss you.
Oh, how the air would be excruciatingly heavy, longing for your return.
But what if I never get to feel this way again?
What if you were it for me?
And I gave up.
I was never patient.
I don't know how I would manage with all those feelings of regret.
Am I willing to take the risk just to be free?

Let's not pretend like you didn't crush every bone in my body.
That one day in 2013 when you refused to admit you cared for me.
I knew you lied...
I pushed, I pried, and I cried.
I sometimes wonder if you only did it to protect me.
I gave you every chance to admit your feelings for me.
I invited the good, the bad, the ugly into our affinity.
I know, I'm not innocent in all of this.
But let's not pretend like some of it wasn't pure bliss.
It was never about feeling safe, even when you towered over me.
It was the way you always made it a point to be soft with me.
I remember asking you years later if you had been in love with me.
A simple yes, and an avalanche of emotions swept over me.
I still felt your connection despite the Atlantic between us.
All I ever wanted was for you to take a chance on us.
But for some reason, I never felt like I was enough.
Just your second cup.

I recall the tears streaming down my cheeks,
Such a salty substance that eventually reached
My quivering lips with those three words, haunting,
The rest of me and the forced words just wanting
To end the whole ordeal
"I never cared" pronounced
Properly even with the difficulties in my heart, I renounced
My position in his life, and witnessed his heartbreak
Right in front of me, a man who couldn`t shake
The feeling that those words I muttered were lies,
Saw his whole life crash in front of my eyes
My most profound emotions hidden in a bottomless pit,
My insecurities taking control all because I couldn`t admit
To him or I that trust was lacking in all aspects,
Of our once perfect relationship with so many defects,
His inability to comprehend my thoughts provoked,
The three little words that had "soulmates" revoked.

I wonder what goes through your mind when someone mentions my name.
It wouldn't surprise me if you never told anyone about me though.
So better yet, I hope every time you meet a woman named Stephanie, it tastes bitter on your tongue, and you can't bring yourself to call her.
If you read a book with a character that resembles me, I hope your heart swells and sinks so deep, your stomach has no room to digest it.
Every time you see me in a crowd, I hope it stops you dead in your tracks and you find yourself gasping for air, just to get a clear view of the woman that isn't me.
You can keep telling yourself that you've been steady since you met me but your core and consistent are refutable.
You haven't had a good night's sleep since you've met me because you've been conflicted ever since.
But it isn't my supposed ill intentions that has you tossing and turning.
It isn't the fact that I was on your sidelines with my heart on my sleeve.
It was that you couldn't handle the fact that someone got close, close enough to hurt you
And it all happened under your nose.
You hated that I knew you, that even when you lied, I could sense it.
I stayed loyal despite the stab wounds on my back.
But the difference now is, since you hung me out to bleed dry, I remain a skeleton in your closet while you're just a ghost from the past
And I don't believe in ghosts.

Subtly.
Subliminally.
Subconsciously.
You remind me that loving you with expectations isn't the true nature of love.
Even if it's with good intentions.
If I can't accept you one hundred percent as you are now, flaws and all, with no hopes for change
But embracing the evolution as it comes
Then I'm not in love with you but the potential of you.
This is the lesson all along.

I told someone about you today; the way we met, how I knew I'd love you the second I saw you and how fate intertwined our souls to constantly mesh despite the distance, the silence, the drunk calls, and the midnight blocks.
The way we'd find our way back to each other, but you were never truly attainable.
He said, "Wow. That's a sweet love story."
I questioned, "Is it? Isn't it kind of sad?"
How we never truly were anything more than colliding cars and crashing hearts.
For years, you had been my forever love, my potential future, and yet still my accepted defeat.

You gave me the big three.

The mental stimulation.

The emotional connection.

The physical chemistry.

You gave me the big O.

With everyone else,

I had to build the mental.

I had to develop the emotional.

I had to gain the physical.

With you, it was instantaneous.

You walked into my place of work and my heart was in my throat.

I felt it pulsating in my fingertips, it made my toes curl.

I had tremors, I was nervous, and you were everything.

Everyone in one fell swoop.

I have never loved anyone that way.

I have never loved anyone that long.

Maybe I'm not in love with you but in love with your memory.

In love with the past.

In love with the potential.

In love with the possibilities.

I hate that we never even tried.

That's all we were,

potential possibilities.

Maybe I never loved you at all.

Maybe I just loved the chase,

The way that I could never call you mine,

The way that we fell apart as fast as we fell together.

How I always wanted to make it right
I just wanted to turn it around.
Maybe I'm still chasing a dream, a fairy-tale,
a potential possibility.

I said I love you.
But I real y hope it wasn't love. It couldn't be.
How could I possibly love someone who would treat me this badly?

LETTING THEM GO

Whether it's an unlocked door,
a small crack in the window or
a ladder leading directly to my heart
you'll always be the lingering wind that can blow open all my vessels.

My deepest secret is that I deny
Deny that I like the chaos of retrogrades.
The mess, the fire, the fury, all its darkness.
The test of communication, time, and patience.
The way Mercury goes in reverse and
I'm stuck moving backward to match.
But in all the misconceptions, I know
I'll cross paths with you again.
The reappearance of an ex-lover is what I look forward to the most.
Because you were my greatest love, my deepest heartbreak but the growth was real.
The developed maturity aligned perfectly, in retrospect.
I was meant to drown in the deep waters.
Rebirth my soul, my energy is anew now.
We are so different, maybe we could be different this time.
I wait for you in retrogrades, within all the mayhem, I hope you find me.
Let's walk through, braver than ever, together.
Hand in hand.
I'll always be where you last left me.

LETTING THEM GO

I close my eyes and it's as if you never left.
Your fingers crawling all over me even if you're nowhere near.
Your love lingers around me like a dark cloud hovering over the night sky _
Just waiting to pour.
You're nestled deep into my shadow.
You're constantly surrounding me.
I can't rid myself of you, even if I tried.

Maybe it's best I love you from a distance.
Every time I get close, you get distant.
I've done it before, and I can do it again.
I'm not exactly sure how this will end.

You kept telling me not to force it.
That we would be whatever we were meant to be.
But is fate all an illusion
for people who aren't willing to put in the time and effort to create a life they've always wanted?
We can't be what we want if we always remain what we already are.

You'd always say, stay true to those who stay true to you
I was always truthful; I was an open book.
I can't be vulnerable if you're not receptive to it.
I can't keep being honest if you're totally against it.
Mostly if you're willing to be everything except more.

It's a full moon and I'm in my feelings.

I'm feeling sensitive, I want to cry and you're the first person that comes to mind.

Maybe I do need you?

A mouth filled with unsent messages.

Deleted before delivery.

Thoughts filled with doubts.

A stream of insecurities you cannot correct.

He loves me, he loves me not.

A shrug of the shoulder.

You're cold and distant.

Maybe, maybe not.

I overthink you.

I am shunned out.

I should find a new home.

But I come back to the one I've always known.

You want me to tell you that
I've changed my mind
I've come to my senses
I want marriage and kids
Despite never wanting that for myself
That I'd love you enough to give you those things
But all I want is for you to love me without those things
Without knowing what I could give to you

Normally
I'd want someone to support my dreams.
Motivate me to attain them.
Inspire me to create new ones.
Recognize my successes,
Congratulate me for them.
Even the smallest ones.

Instead
He says, "I guess I had higher expectations of you than you had for yourself."

Rather than
Trying to convince him otherwise.
Getting emotional over the phone.
Questioning my worth.
Feeling belittled.
Inferior.

I should have said, "Ditto."

He says, "What about you has changed exactly?"

I should have said, "This is why I don't like you. How did I ever fall in love with you?"

I should have said, "Fuck you!"

Dial tone.

So here it is...
Fuck you!

LETTING THEM GO

You used to make me cry with your razor blade words.
Quick slip of the tongue,
Sudden thunder and a heart-sinking into nothingness.

Let go.
Let go of the past.
Let go of the potential.
Let go of the memories.
Let go of the false reality.

Let go of what you think he made you feel.

Forgive for the illusions.
Forgive for the past.
Forgive for the holding on.
Forgive for letting go.

Let go of the dreams.
The fantasy that he`ll come back.
Come back and fight to make it right.
Fight to make it work.
Fight to have you back.

Let go and live.
Live for you.
Love for you.
Learn for you.
Laugh for you.

LETTING THEM GO

Stop the vicious cycle.
Stop the vicious circle.
Stop the rotation.
Stop letting go and holding onto hope.
Choose to let go.
Or choose to hold on.
But you can't do both.
My vote is with letting go.

We were taught to never say never.
I taught myself to never say always.

Marshmallow

You said I love you and welcomed me into your heart.
I built a home in the comfort of it all, with you as my counterpart.
I love you, without the too.
I had four white walls and a beautiful red roof.
The beating of your metronome was the needed proof.
As long as it kept beating for me _
In my house of hearts, I could sleep
Freely.
But then the nightmares started, and I had no escape.
You caused an avalanche that I tried to fix with tape.
In the end, my home broke down to pieces
And I realized that the basis of our foundation had all these diseases.

It's interesting how respect works.
It's like being polite with little quirks.
You say you feel terrible for what you did,
despite keeping the dirty little secret that you hid.
The first person that shows interest and you commit.
There's a million girls you could fuck with, I admit
But the fact that you're keeping her around
Knowing what you did
Knowing that she caused me so much pain
it's like carrying around luggage with a bloody knife,
it's just so fucking inhumane.
So, although you feel terrible, not enough to disrespect me more.
I swear it shocks me to my very core
I would have put my hand on fire to guarantee
You'd never stoop so low to disrespect me.

One glance from her and the rapid heart race to the finish line.
You probably knew you'd cheat your way out of this one.
You did the one thing I would never forgive you for _
and it's fine.
Is it self-sabotage, if it's not your battleship?
I deserved better, I deserved more.
You always had a way of sneaking up on me.
This time you crashed into me like a wave hits the shore.
But it's just like you to leave in the middle of a tsunami.

Nightmares creeping up.
I got middle of the night insomnia.
Steph, something must be wrong with ya
Fighting the urge to text him every other day.
Why, why not?
He loves me, he loves me not -
All the other ones I wasn't friends with.
But for four years, he was my best friend.
I wish there was a different end.
All mixed in love.
There's a lot of love left _
There's a lot of love in me left.
But the love is for the loss of a friend.
RIP to the bestie.
You were literally everything to me.
And you say you'll miss me.
I wonder if it's me or just the company.

Lump in my throat
Pin in my heart
Emptiness in my stomach
I feel everything.
It all gets to be too much.
Eventually, I feel numb.
I feel nothing at all _
Just empty.
I swallow the lump.
My heart is deflated like a balloon.
I need some air
I can't catch my breath.
This feels like death.
Anxiety is my new best friend.
She is there in place of love _
In place of him.
So many firsts _
And just one end.
No turning back.
Because done is done _
when it's over, it's over.
I hate this four-letter word the most.

Maybe I'm not unblocked.
Maybe it's better that way.
I know I said I wouldn't text you but
Today is ruined anyway.
From one old friend to another, I'm definitely not okay.
I wish you were here; I wish you could hold me.
Then disappear.
Seems like I'll always be someone's life lesson
Never someone's happy ending.

It's upsetting to know you're not even allowing yourself to process everything, you're just forcing yourself to move on. Why won't you let your feelings for me fade instead of suppressing them? They'll come back, in the long run, either way. You say you've wasted a month by not feeling better and entertaining my messages. I say I wasted the last year of our relationship because I didn't just leave instead of entertaining your empty effort. You're the one that did me wrong and I'm the one left chasing you. When I slow down and think about it, I'm chasing answers that I'll never get and you're just in the way. You say you love me, but you're begging for me to leave you alone. I wonder how you can still love me and yet be so quick to let me go. It's only been a month since we called it quits and you're already fucking over it, while I am struggling to find my way. But I know that down the road, I'll be on my path, and you'll probably be making the same mistakes.

Phoenix

A year ago,

I deleted my Snapchat, deactivated my IG and my Facebook, called two of my best friends and mother to tell them the news...
I went from being a full-time girlfriend and a part-time stepmother for 4 years to bawling my eyes out because I, once again, "failed."

I had to pack all my bags while studying for exams, find somewhere to live on a part-time income, pay for movers to move my stuff out of the apartment we shared as quickly as possible, say goodbye to a child that I learned to love as if she were my own, and leave a second, third, fourth, family behind.

The amicable and mutual decision to end our relationship made me realize that I had been forcing myself to work on it for the last year instead of coming to terms with the fact that I honestly was unhappy. I didn't feel appreciated. I didn't feel loved. I was depressed. He knew this, I knew this. I was constantly giving all my energy to a relationship that was bleeding me dry. I forced myself to love at 100% even though I saw none of that love come back. I didn't fight anymore because I didn't care, I was numb to it all. I was tired of repeating myself. I had consistently put him, his daughter, and his family above everything.

I believe the tears, at first, were a sign of relief. I escaped. I finally felt free. But the relationship ending didn't hit me as hard as losing my best friend. Or the person I thought was my best friend. In the last year of our relationship, the love disappeared but the friendship remained. We talked, we laughed, we shared jokes, secrets, feelings. But then I found out that he had cheated, and it blew my whole freedom out of the water. I was back to questioning myself and all the time, energy, love, and effort I put into that relationship. I begged him for answers. I begged him to stop seeing her. I begged him to tell me why. I begged him to explain how he didn't even respect me enough as a girlfriend, as a friend, as a person to break up with me first. I'm such an understanding person, I would have been hurt but I would have understood. I was losing my mind because I couldn't believe that someone that I had trusted for so long would stoop so low and then lie to my face about it. I lost my confidence, my self-worth, my ability to see the light at the end of the tunnel. All I wanted to do was sleep. My willingness and motivation to go to work and finish school were gone. I went on medical leave from work without pay, I went to therapy, I was put on antidepressants. I literally cried for no reason and all reasons. I literally cried everywhere and anywhere. I had hit rock bottom.

I didn't realize at the time that I was getting all the toxins out of my body. I was releasing myself from all the negativity, all the stress, all the pressure, all the empty words, absent actions, and broken promises. I was ridding myself completely of all the failed attempts to make it work. I was forgiving him so I could be at peace, and I was forgiving myself for letting him treat me like I was nothing. I was addressing all the emotions as they appeared, diving deep into each other, accepting them, and then letting them form into tears so they could escape me.

At one point, I stopped crying. I stopped questioning myself. I stopped begging for answers. I stopped begging him to show me the respect that I so clearly deserved. Once everything was moved out, and I had said my goodbyes, I realized that I hadn't failed. I wasn't a failure because my relationship failed. I wasn't worthless because someone else couldn't recognize my value. My life didn't stop because my relationship ended, and I still had my whole life ahead of me. I am still young, I am still strong, I am still beautiful. My ability to love didn't disappear just because someone wasn't able to love me back. I came out on top.

A year later,

After some extremely supportive friends and family let me vent all my sorrows and a lot of visits to my amazing Godson...

I am now living on my own and just a few short months from graduating with a bachelor's degree. I still have my health, my laugh, my courage, my love, and my determination. I have a roof over my head, a job that pays all my bills on time, food in the fridge, and neighbors that let me use their washer and dryer (Shoutout to my brother and his girlfriend).

I know that Thanksgiving was yesterday, but I wanted to wait until today to say that I am so thankful for all my experiences, my struggles, my failures, and my lessons learned. I am thankful that I can keep getting knocked down and continue to get back up. I am thankful that people walking out of my life has never stopped me from opening the door to new opportunities and possibilities. I am thankful for being reminded that I shouldn't ignore my wants and needs just to satisfy someone else's. I am thankful for realizing that sometimes I must save myself instead of trying to save everyone else. I can only hope that I continue to be as resilient as I was in the last year. Thank you, life, for reminding me that you are always 10 steps ahead.

Checkmate!

www.ingramcontent.com/pod-product-compliance
Lightning Source LLC
Chambersburg PA
CBHW030043100526
44590CB00011B/313